# THE POWER TO SUCCEED

*Unlock Your Life, Unlock Your Dreams*

**SHIRLEY BROWN DANZY**

Copyright © 2022 by Shirley Brown Danzy

Published by Shirley Brown Danzy in Partnership with
**Bold Publishing**
(https://denisenicholson.com/bold-publishing)

Book Cover by: Bold Publishing
Book Layout by: Opeyemi Ikuborije

**Publisher's Note:**

Without limiting the rights under copyright reserved above, no part of this publication may be reproduced, stored in or introduced into a retrieval system, or transmitted, in any form, or by any means (electronic, mechanical, photocopying, recording, or otherwise), without the prior written permission of both the copyright owner and the publisher of the book.

Manufactured in the United States of America

ISBN: 978-1-7363853-9-5

Library of Congress Control Number: 2022912625

Follow Shirley Brown Danzy

**Social Media Outlets:**
Facebook: https://m.facebook.com/?_rdr
Instagram: @authorshirleybrowndanzy
Email: shirleybrowndanzy.com

CONTENTS

*Dedication* . . . . . . . . . . . . . . . . . . . . . . . . . . . . . . . . . . . . . . . . . . . *i*
*Foreword* . . . . . . . . . . . . . . . . . . . . . . . . . . . . . . . . . . . . . . . . . . *iii*
*Acknowledgment* . . . . . . . . . . . . . . . . . . . . . . . . . . . . . . . . . . . *vii*

Introduction . . . . . . . . . . . . . . . . . . . . . . . . . . . . . . . . . . . . . . . . 1

**CHAPTER ONE:** Make an Impact, Make a Difference . . . . . . . . . . 5

**CHAPTER TWO:** Forgiving Self and Others. . . . . . . . . . . . . . . . . . 9

**CHAPTER THREE:** Understanding You
(Clear mental vision of self) . . . . . . . . . . . . . . . . . . . . . . . . . . . . . 15

**CHAPTER FOUR:** The Time I Spent
(Journey to Self-Development) . . . . . . . . . . . . . . . . . . . . . . . . . . 25

**CHAPTER FIVE:** Believing in Yourself . . . . . . . . . . . . . . . . . . . . . 35

**CHAPTER SIX:** Develop your Mind for Greatness. . . . . . . . . . . . . 41

**CHAPTER SEVEN:** Time to Act . . . . . . . . . . . . . . . . . . . . . . . . . . 45

**CHAPTER EIGHT:** Shift your Mindset. . . . . . . . . . . . . . . . . . . . . 51

**CHAPTER NINE:** Finding your Divine Purpose, your Gift. . . . . . . 57

**CHAPTER TEN:** Aligning Vision to Divine Purpose............61

**Chapter Eleven:** Checking your Envy........................69

**Chapter Twelve:** Developing Calmness of Mind................71

**Chapter Thirteen:** Becoming Resilient and Driven
(Staying focused on your true purpose).......................87

**Chapter Fourteenth:** Celebrating You.......................91

About the Author............................................97

More About the Author.......................................99

Note Pages-My Plan for Success.............................106

# Dedication

This book is dedicated to my late father, John D Brown, and my mother, Essie M. Brown who both taught me to always stretch myself to learn more and to be an independent and determined person. I appreciate you both for your many years of love, dedication and support; and for introducing me to the spiritual world. I am who I am today because of your patience, love and guidance. You taught me to get up when I fell down and to stay focused and go after my dreams. The love I have for you both will forever live on in my heart, mind and soul. I pray that my journey through life will serve as a reminder to others of how well you instilled values within me that will continue to serve others and make the world a little brighter. I am Shirley Brown, the daughter of John D and Essie Brown.

# Foreword

You have something special; you have greatness in you. I'm Les Brown, this is a time where people are looking for keys, steps and methods that will allow them to navigate this new place where we are, in and out of a pandemic. A book that I highly recommend that you get is entitled, "*The Power to Succeed*," because you do have the power to do that.

This book is designed to help you unlock the life that's waiting for you to live and therefore, have access to unlocking your dreams. It has been said that most people die at age 25 and don't get buried until they are 65. The late Dr. Myles Munroe said something very important. He said, "The graveyard is the richest place on the surface of the earth because there you will see the books that were not published, ideas that were not harnessed, songs that were not sung, and drama pieces that were never acted." **Rob the cemetery, of your gifts, talents, abilities, and your dreams.**

*The Power to Succeed* allows you to do just that. Each chapter is designed to give you the keys to begin to unlock the unlimited potential in you, to do more and to have more.

I am reminded of the words in Lion King, "Simba, you are more than that, which you have become." In this book, *The Power to Succeed* you will realize as you begin to discover the life in you that has been waiting for you to step up, that you are more than that which you have become. You begin to become a grave robber and begin to live your dreams rather than your fears.

This is a book I highly recommend. Shirley is serious. She has put a book together that is going to change your life. I encourage you to read it, recommend it to family members and friends, and get ready to succeed at a whole new level; on 'steroids.' Get ready to unlock your life and your dreams. I'm Les Brown, Ms. Mamie Brown's baby boy, that's my story, and I'm sticking to it.

Yours in GREATNESS,
Les Brown
Speaker, Author, Trainer

"The world is waiting for you to wake up to the person you are called to be. Stop listening to the negative inner conversation that's causing you to play small. Focus your mind on positive thoughts, possibilities and solutions that can move you forward. Tap into your creativity and determination and stay busy.

Stay focused."— **Les Brown**

### Success: If You Want It Bad Enough

"If you want a thing bad enough to go out and fight for it,
to work day and night for it,
to give up your time, your peace and your sleep for it, if all
that you dream and scheme is about it,
and life seems useless and worthless without it,
if you gladly sweat for it, and fret for it, and plan for it, and
lose all your terror of the opposition for it,
if you simply go after that thing that you want with all of
your capacity, strength and sagacity, faith, hope and
confidence, and stern pertinacity, if neither cold, poverty,
famine, nor gout, sickness nor pain, of body and brain,
can keep you away from the thing that you want, if dogged
and grim you beseech and beset it, with the help of God, you
will surely get it!"

—by Berton Braley—

# Acknowledgment

This book would not have been possible without the help and support of my dear family, relatives, friends, Les Brown and the Power Voice Community, Jon Talarico and the Thinking into Results Community, and Dr. Denise Nicholson and the Writing Incubator Community.

Mike A. Smith, former Major League Baseball player and father of my children, I thank you for your patience and understanding as I worked diligently on this book. I appreciate your support, time, and commitment.

To my children, Jeremy, Janae, Bridney, and Michael, thank you for your love, support, understanding, and just being there when I needed someone to listen or give me a break for relaxation.

Thanks to my dear sisters and brothers, John E., Walter, Emma, and Vertis, for your unselfish love and dedicated support for so many years, and your understanding during my book writing journey.

I want to thank my paternal grandparents, the late Julius Brown Sr. and Bessie Love Brown, for being such great role models to follow and for demonstrating the importance of family and spirituality throughout their lives. I thought of them both as I wrote, page after page.

I also want to thank my maternal grandmother, the late Corene Young, my late aunt, Bessie Brown and Earlean Brown Terry, for being there for me and sharing their years of wisdom. Your memories guided my pen as I wrote, word after word.

To my children's paternal grandparents, Jessie Sulton and Elnora Osborne, paternal aunt Jimme Sulton and uncle Walter Smith; thanks so much for the kind words, support and words of wisdom that inspired my thoughts as I put pen to paper, chapter by chapter.

To my cousin, Teresa Key, who has always been like a sister to me; I thank you for being there for me to bounce my ideas off during my writing journey. You never got tired of listening.

To my many other dear aunts, uncles, nieces, nephews, sisters-in-law, brother-in-law, cousins, and friends, thank you for so many years of support, laughter, and dedication. You are appreciated.

Special thanks to Dr. Denise Nicholson, my writing coach, accountability partner, the owner of the Writing Incubator program, and CEO of Bold Publishing Company. Dr. Denise Nicholson, thank you for being there at every step of my writing journey. You have been truly remarkable and committed to each writing incubator challenge community member. You were dedicated to helping each member successfully get the words out of their head and onto paper. Thank you for your dedication and support during my writing journey; you made it so much easier for me to complete my book. I appreciate you and your unselfish commitment to excellence.

Special thanks to Jon Talarico, who is considered among the world's foremost experts in building relationships. Jon is known by many as "The Connector." Through Jon's program, I connected with the right people to make my book-writing journey a success.

Special thanks to my mentor and voice coach, Les Brown, who has been named one of the top five speakers in the world. Les Brown, thank you for your undying commitment to your craft and your endless desire to share your gift with me, and so many others. You are truly a remarkable human being. Thank you so much for coaching me to develop my power voice and for writing the foreword for my first book of resiliency, encouragement, inspiration, and motivation.

# Introduction

*"If you are not willing to learn, no one can help you. If you are determined to learn, no one can stop you."*—**Zig Ziglar**

My eyes were fixed on the windowpane, watching for a sign to confirm my direction, my destiny, my path. I sat alone in the room that was so quiet and still. My mind wandered, on and on, to dreams that seemed so real. Why do I keep seeing the same visions? What meaning do they have? I long to be successful but yet I'm stuck in my path. At the windowpane I still stare, waiting for my sign. I know my dreams are possible, but doubt and fear keep coming to my mind.

When I hear people talk about their dreams for success, their ambition to shock the world and leave their mark, I smile because I know dreams really do come true if only we believe, plan and are willing to act toward their attainment.

Everyone yearns for health, happiness, security, peace of mind and true expression, but many fail to achieve clearly defined results. I know how deep our thoughts run when we are trying to establish a better life for ourselves and for our families. Believe me, I have been there. The good thing is, our success starts with a thought.

Albert Einstein said, "Imagination is everything. It is the preview of life's coming attractions." I believe he meant that our imagination shows us what our true purpose is; our life to come. *The Law of Success*, lesson six, by Napoleon Hill indicates that imagination is an essential ingredient for success. It is during our childhood that we develop our imagination, but when we become adults, we often forget how creative our imagination was during our childhood. Who we really are is still there. It is time to stop just surviving and begin to truly live.

As a child, you believed your thoughts. However, society, our families, our friends and associates started telling us to stop believing in our thoughts. So, we felt compelled to stop. When we stop listening to our thoughts, we become unhappy, we become depressed.

Somewhere along our journey through life, we forgot about the visions we had. We stopped dreaming; we simply became stuck in the midst of our journey. We began to struggle to find our purpose in life. I am reminded of Myles Munroe, "Your success is your purpose. Until you find it, you will never be satisfied."

The Merriam-Webster dictionary defines vision as "something seen in a dream, trance, or ecstasy, a supernatural appearance that conveys a revelation; a thought, concept, or object formed by the imagination". It defines imagination as the "act, process, or power of forming a mental picture of something not present and especially of something a person has not known or experienced". When we think of our dreams, the quest for our true purpose often takes us back to our childhood days; back to the daydreams we had that brought smiles to our faces and happiness in our hearts, minds, and souls. We each have our own view of what happiness and abundance is for us. Only we can see the fullness of it through our visions. Go back and find your childhood dreams; that is who you truly are.

Many have aligned Albert Einstein's quote with the scripture, "Faith is the substance of things hoped for, the evidence of things not seen" (Hebrew 11:1 KJV). So, yet again we see this idea of imagination. I believe this scripture tells us to pay close attention to the things we imagine; the things we want so badly that we hope for them, wanting them to come into fruition. Our imagination is a preview of what is to come for us in life. The power to succeed begins in our imagination.

Some people claim their imaginations run wild. They think of so many things that they can't narrow down their true gift. To find your true gift, your true purpose, you must pay close attention to the things that fascinate you, the things that catch your interest and attention. Focus on the things you imagine over and over again. On the other hand, many people know exactly what they want in life, and what their gift is. They have figured it out.

Have you ever talked to someone and felt the positive energy they brought with each spoken word? They were full of passion and enthusiasm as they told you about the events of their story. You became excited and joyful just listening to them. Their energy and passion uplifted you. You had to pause and say, "They must love what they do!"

Now, take a minute to remember what games and activities you enjoyed as a child or as a teenager that brought you this same excitement, enthusiasm and fulfillment. Follow your journey through life, paying close attention to the things you were so passionate about and enjoyed so much that you would lose track of time. Make a list of all these things.

Another key activity that I recommend is to ask your close friends, family members and co-workers to name one or two things they feel you do well. You are looking for your strengths. Write them on your list.

The key to realizing our true purpose lies in our ability to review our unique list, assess our strengths, come up with a plan, act, and check to see what is working in terms of moving us closer to our goals, dreams and success.

To have the things we desire, the things we want in life, we have to keep an open mind and be willing to learn the power of the mind.

If you truly desire more and are determined to learn, as Zig Ziglar said, "no one can stop you". My hope is to help as many people as possible to realize they can live the life they have dreamed about. This book will guide you through life experiences with quotes and stories to help you connect your thoughts to your divine purpose. We only get one chance to live here on earth; why not find the passcode to unlock your life and your dreams so that you can live a life full of purpose and abundance? We all deserve this.

CHAPTER ONE

# Make an Impact, Make a Difference

*"We were placed on earth to fulfill a purpose, and that purpose is what gives meaning to our lives, you were sent to the world to make an impact and make a difference"* —**Myles Munroe**

I sat in my car today eating lunch when out of nowhere, a huge bird appeared. It was flying very low and in circles. I sat there and I thought about all the circles I seemed to be walking in throughout my life. The bird made four huge circles in the sky and then on the last loop, he struggled to get enough momentum to get high enough to fly farther. I sat and watched as it continued to fly up and drop down repeatedly.

I do not know what the bird's struggle was; perhaps it was not feeling well. What I did know was that the bird was having a difficult time trying to stay up in the clear, blue sky. I noticed that although it struggled, it did not give up. The bird did not fly to the ground to rest for a moment. It continued to struggle and struggle to move further north as though someone, or something, was calling or waiting on it.

As I watched the bird, I thought about my dreams and the many challenges I had faced on my journey to greatness. I too must be like that bird, never quitting and continuing to fly higher and higher until I reach my destiny.

I often hear people say that your *why*, your *reason*, will give you the energy and the heart to continue to push on in spite of the adversity or roadblocks you encounter. Do you ever lie awake wondering just what went wrong and how you got to where you are today? I challenge you today to ask yourself what your reason is for wanting more. Then think about what caused you to stop dreaming and taking action to pursue those wants, those dreams. What visions of happiness have you seen play out repeatedly in your imagination? What gives your heart joy and excitement and fills your very soul with fire, happiness, and ambition? Take a moment and write it down.

There is power in taking the time to simply write your visions down. I believe that for us to begin our journey to success, we must reposition our minds for greatness. We must write the vision and put it in a place where we will see it often, as a reminder to keep moving in our direction of success and impact.

What impact will you make during the one life you have to live? Are you the person who will be willing to go all in to live the life you have dreamed about?

Motivational Speaker Les Brown said, "I believe there are three kinds of people. There are winners, who know what they want and understand their potential and the possibilities, they take life on. Next are losers, who don't have a clue as to who they are. They allow circumstances to shape their lives and their self-image. I believe there is a third group as well. This consists of potential winners whose lives are just slightly out of alignment. I call them wayward winners. It may be that they just need to learn how to be real winners. Perhaps they've hit a bump or two that has knocked them off course and they are temporarily befuddled."

Which of these three kinds of people are you?

CHAPTER TWO

# Forgiving Self and Others

*"In order to heal we must* **first forgive**… *And sometimes the person we must forgive is* **ourselves**" —**Mila Bron**

**Forgiving Self and Others.** It is so hard to move forward when you have not released yourself from your past; all the stuff that keeps coming to mind that keeps dragging you down. The guilt, shame, disappointments, all the people who have wronged you, things you wish you could do over, changing what you did, where you went, or the actions you took in the past.

You hate that feeling of anxiety in your stomach, the replay that runs through your mind over and over. Deep down, you feel sick just thinking about what you did and what you should have done and how you are going to correct it. I believe we all have been there. You wish you could go back and get another opportunity to do things differently. You beat yourself up over it. Maybe you forgot a special person's birthday, told something you should not have shared, gone somewhere you felt you should not have gone, or wronged someone who had caused you no harm.

The guilt and shame we feel can cause us to become stuck in the moment if we don't recognize these actions for what they are, mistakes. We often don't take the time to acknowledge that in those moments, we were merely trying to figure things out as we encountered trial after trial.

To become unstuck, we must find the courage to let go of the guilt and shame that comes as a result of going against our personal value system. Whenever we go against our morals and values, it creates a mental struggle to try to justify our actions and try to right the wrong we have done.

But are we being fair to ourselves by holding on to the worst parts of our journey? I believe we are not. No matter what it is that keeps running through your mind, know that it is not just a problem for you; the desire to go back and do things differently is a desire for all of us in some unique way. Unfortunately, life does not give us this privilege, but it does give us the opportunity to learn from the mistakes that have caused us pain, resentment, and heartache.

Nevertheless, it is important to recognize that it is through the difficult times that we change, we become better versions of ourselves. The challenges that cause us so much pain, so many sleepless nights, so much anxiety, also shape us to become more powerful, stronger, more resilient, and wiser human beings.

True power lies in our understanding that trouble does not last always. Through this knowledge we understand that when we face trials, it is not the end for our destiny. It is simply a test of our character, our values, and morals. We are not in control of those we face but we are in control of how we react to the situations we encounter.

Difficult times harden you, and make you think longer and quicker than when you are calmed by good times. No known formula for fulfillment will work for you if you do not have the "will to win"—the desire to live a life of fulfillment, the desire to want to be a success of some kind. While you may have desire, you will be moving in circles if you do not have some "know how" to advise your wishes in life.

Many people have attained success merely because trouble propelled them on, made them so mad, that it gave them the drive and energy to make up their minds that they were going to be a success, no matter what.

Appreciate the tough times. Even though it is hard, welcome trouble. It triggers you. Of course, you have to know when success has arrived, so pay attention. Knowing how to recognize success when it comes is an important phase on your journey to success.

In the midst of our trials, we must acknowledge when we mess up, own up to our mistakes and keep going. It is easy to make excuses to try to smooth things over, but after so many excuses you lose credibility with people and lose confidence in yourself. People stop trusting us and our words lose their power. When our words lose value, we lose value.

We have to seek value in each interaction and honor our word. The best way to heal and get your life back on track is to be honest with yourself. Admit what was done wrong, right as many of the wrongs as you possibly can and apologize to those you have wronged.

Some will accept your apology right away, if they feel it is sincere. Others may take a while to come around, it is okay. Give them space and time.

Knowing that you have done all you can to right the wrongs, you can begin to forgive yourself and move on. As we grow through each challenge, we become more resilient. Start today, right now, forgive all things, bless it, and push forward. Realize that no one is perfect, and that life is a journey filled with joy, peace, happiness and pain.

I have always found comfort in focusing on the good old days and moments in time that brought me simple joy, pure joy. What are those thoughts for you? Once you choose your moments, hold those thoughts. Allow them to dim the negative thoughts that will come to mind from time to time. You will need the good moments to distract you from the thoughts that will hinder your growth. You must learn how to shift your mindset.

Remember that all that stuff, the regrets and the pain, distract you from living the life you imagined. Negative distractions have caused wasted time and energy for so many people.

I challenge you today to release yourself from repetitive anxiety and guilt, use that energy to fuel your dream, your passion, and your unique gift. Once you know better, you must do better and keep moving forward, do not look back. Some people feel that they just cannot move on. It is important to know that you can, and you must. You can begin by surrounding yourself with like-minded, positive people. Negative-minded people will drain positive energy from you. Positive-minded people energize and encourage success in themselves and others. You will need uplifting from time to time.

I do not begin to know, or make little, of your challenges, your obstacles, or your setbacks. It is not my place to do that. What I do know is you have to find a way to make peace with it and move on. If it takes therapy, love yourself enough to get the help you need and deserve.

I have found that some people look for the good in every situation and some people look for the bad. The people who look for the good give off positive energy. The people who look for the bad give off negative energy. Learning how to shift the conversation is a valuable communication technique to stay positive and productive and on your path to your destiny.

My favorite mentor, Les Brown, said, "Ask for help not because you are weak but because you want to remain strong". Your pursuit of happiness deserves that from you. You have to do it for yourself and the people you love. The way we think, our mood, and our energy affects everyone and everything around us. So, take the time to get the healing you deserve.

"Forgiveness is not a one off decision;
it is a journey and a process
that takes time, determination, and
persistence. Forgiveness is not forgetting;
it is simply denying your pain
the right to control your life."

—**Corallie Buchanan**

CHAPTER THREE

# Understanding You
# (Clear mental vision of self)

*"Self-awareness is the ability to take an honest look at your life without any attachment to it being right or wrong, good or bad"*
—Debbie Ford.

**The Power of self-awareness is the starting point to self-discovery.** When we become aware of our true selves, we experience a sense of freedom; a freeing of the mind, body, and spirit. I cannot begin to express the full magnitude of the experience.

I once heard someone relate their experience of self-actualization to climbing a mountain and getting to the top after enduring challenges along the way. There were times when they felt like giving up, but they found the will to continue. Once they made it to the top, there was a feeling of overwhelming joy, peace and accomplishment that you can only appreciate after the journey of your climb. No one else can experience the full magnitude and impact of the trials that you have overcome throughout your journey unless they too have climbed the mountain of self-discovery, and even then, their unique experience would still be different from your own. In essence, we can share our journey through our story, but not the experience.

This is how you feel when you become one with who you are. You no longer worry about what others think or feel about you. You are comfortable in your own skin. You own the space you fill with confidence and boldness; your presence makes a statement. Once we become aware of whom we really are, the growing process flourishes and we begin to align with our unique purpose.

When we gain the capacity to learn from our mistakes, as well as our successes and experiences along the way, we gain the inner strength to keep going. We begin to see a much larger version of ourselves and of our potential. We understand that we deserve to live a life that will outlive us.

We now know that no matter where we start in life, anything is possible if we merely believe and work toward its attainment. We know that we are truly in charge of our destiny.

We no longer seek to blame others; rather, we seek opportunities that will propel us closer to our dreams and goals. We are in charge of our own destiny, and we know that it is up to us to give it the time and energy it deserves.

Many people go through life wanting more, yet still giving up and settling for what is within their immediate environment. I do not believe in settling any more. I have come to realize that the true power that people need is already within them. We are given so many signs, so many visions, but we overlook them and choose things that bring us temporary satisfaction, temporary joy. We lose sight of the true prize.

I was sitting in my room and reflecting over my life one night, trying to figure out how to shift my life from normal to extraordinary. I thought, as I sat there, that I too, deserved for my dreams to come true. I too, deserved to live the life I had dreamt about, the life that gave me meaning, value and abundance.

I kept wondering how I was going to do it. At age 54 I sat there thinking of so many wasted years, so much time spent doing things that would not get me closer to my dream. I spent time looking at people around me who were not playing by the rules and their actions were affecting my success. I was doing things to please others and putting myself last. I had to just tell myself to stop! Stop worrying about things and people over whom I had no control. I was wasting valuable energy on trying to figure out why other people were allowing the system to be broken and unfair and stood by as though they could not see it.

In bed one night, a thought came to mind. "Stop worrying over it! Focus on you. What is meant for you, you will have, and no one can take it from you, and no one can stop you from achieving it." From that moment on, I made it my business to focus on the things I could control. I decided, in that moment, to spend my time and energy on developing myself. I realized that I had to stop giving my power away to others and use all my power to propel my life forward. It was the best decision I could have ever made. I said to myself, "It is time for me to work on me."

I was determined to do whatever was required to figure it out. I began listening to motivational speakers such as Les Brown, Lisa Nichols, Eric

Thomas, Mel Robins, Brian Tracy, Steve Harvey, Jim Rohn, and Zig Ziglar and ministers such as T.D. Jakes, Joel Osteen, and Myles Munroe. I found peace, energy, and a renewed excitement within me as I listened to motivation each day. I gained, through their words, the fuel to fire my desire to get back up and go for my dreams. I just needed a little encouragement.

I encourage you to find a motivational speaker and/or minister who also motivates and inspires you to become a better version of yourself. Sometimes we just need a little encouragement to get us back on track.

Start your day off with words that uplift you and keep you focused on your journey to success. It was not too late for me, and it is certainly not too late for you if you are able and willing to run toward your dreams.

Each day, I would listen to Les Brown say, "Do not worry about the how. The how is none of your business". I would listen to Lisa Nichols remind me that "her God is not going to give her, her dream and not give you, your dream." It was through these words, and others, that I found the power to continue to push forward. You have to be the same way. What are the words that will keep you focused on your dreams? You will need to know the words that ignite the greatness within you. You will need these words when self-doubt comes to convince you to give up and turn back to your old ways, back to your comfort zone. Also, take the time each day to think of at least five things you are grateful for. Write them down and reflect on them instead of thinking of the things you don't have.

Through listening to the stories shared by many of these motivational speakers, I found that they took the time to invest in themselves to learn how to be the best in their industry. We must be willing to invest in ourselves. Many of us spend more than we make on material things. This is a mistake. Benjamin Franklin said, "If you empty your purse into your mind, your mind will fill your purse".

Money, just the mere word, has a fascinating sound. In many, it conjures the vision of some kind of delighted fantasy where they see themselves in a make-believe world, where to wish, is to have.

Yet in real life, money brings with it only two characteristics of value: the character it generates in the making and the self-expression of the individuality in the use of it, once it has been made.

The power of using money places a man who has become the captain of his soul, in the process of its acquisition, also in control of the circumstances that surround him.

He can shape his existing world to his liking. Aside from these two faculties, the character in acquisition and power in use, money has hardly any value and is expected to be a curse just as much as it is a blessing. For this reason, the person who has mastered the control of money will oftentimes care little about leaving huge wealth to his descendants.

Wealth without the wish, the mind, or the power to use it is too often the medium through which men gratify the flesh with exceptional living, and the mind with foolishness, until death; operating through carelessness and recklessness which may lead many to an early grave.

The value of money lies, first in the striving for it and then in the use of it.

I was very eager to get started on my journey of self-discovery and mastery of self. I was willing to make the shift from spending money on material things to spending money on developing myself. Don't be afraid to invest in yourself. Invest in your dreams.

I felt if others could accomplish their dreams, then I could accomplish mine. I decided to be all in. I made it my New Year's resolution.

I was sitting at my desk at work when a co-worker approached me and asked if I wanted to attend a candle making class with her. I thought about it for a moment and then replied, "Yes, I can do that because it aligns with my New Year's resolution." She said, "What was your resolution?" I told her that it was to not spend money unless it was an investment in myself to improve my knowledge and skills to make money. I attended the class with her, then I started a candle making business.

As I was making candles and listening to motivation, I kept thinking, *I sure would love Les Brown to teach me how to speak as he does, with power and conviction.* I would often lie awake, dreaming of the moment and surfing the internet looking to see if he offered the opportunity to learn from him. I found his website, lesbrowninstitute.com. I wanted to fill out the interest information but the negative voice in my head said, "You cannot afford him, why are you filling out that form?"

After I started my candle business, a co-worker told me I needed an Instagram page. I went home and asked my daughters how to create one. One of my daughters created the page for me. After she finished it, I clicked the key to follow Les Brown and Lisa Nichols on their Instagram pages.

One day, I was on my Instagram page and saw Les Brown offering a Power Voice training program. The page read, "If you are interested, type Power into the chat box." I could not sleep that night.

I was afraid to even type the word into the box. I asked my family if I should enroll, and they asked how much the program cost. I told them the price and they said no. I went to my friends and asked, and they said that if I wanted to just give some money away, I could give it to them, and they would teach me. I mentioned it to a coworker, and he said, "Shirley, if this is something you truly want to do, I would do it. It is just money; you can make it back. It is an investment in you."

I went home again, and this time I was confused. I prayed over it that night and asked God to give me a sign that would let me know what I should do. I was sitting on the bed and thinking about it and my daughter walked in and said, "Mom, if you really want Les Brown to teach you, you should do it." I smiled and said, "I think I am going to do it."

As I sat there, I also thought of the New Year's resolution I had made in 2019. It was now 2020 but it was not time for me to stop. I realized that it was *my* dream to be mentored by Les Brown. It was not the dream or vision of the people I had asked. There is no way they could understand the impact it would have on my life if he agreed to work with me.

The vision of being taught by him, the person I felt was, and is, the best in the industry, was put in my head, not theirs. I thought, "Why did I waste time asking others what they thought?" I started answering myself, "Was I expecting them to talk me out of it?" I was already about to let fear do that anyway. I was looking for an excuse to stay in my comfort zone.

I enrolled in Les Brown's Power Voice Training, where I met his business consultant, Jon Talarico. I later decided to also study under Jon Talarico to understand my mindset and why I was allowing fear to stop me from reaching my full potential.

Jon offered a course entitled *Thinking Into Results*, as part of the Bob Proctor and Sandy Gallagher Institute. During my 6-month training with Jon, I focused on changing my mindset and becoming aware of myself. For the first time in my life, I could see the pieces of my life coming together like a puzzle. Both programs were worth every single penny and more.

Once enrolled in Les Brown's Power Voice training, I was introduced to others who would help me excel in my business. People like Brian Tracy, Mike Williams, Ian Harvey, Dr. Denise Nicholson and Alicia and Lorette Lytle. He did not just want his students to learn to speak with power and conviction, but he wanted us to have the necessary resources to help us excel in the speaking industry.

Les Brown proved himself to be a remarkable human being who truly wanted to use his gift to help others achieve greatness.

I had imagined being trained by Les Brown and there I was; *being trained by Les Brown*. It all started with a thought.

"The robbers of time
are the past and the future.
Man should bless the past, and
forget it, if it keeps him in bondage, and
bless the future, knowing it has in store for
him endless joys, but live fully in the now."

— **Florence Scovel Shinn**

CHAPTER FOUR

# The Time I Spent
# (Journey to Self-Development)

*"When life brings you full circle, pay attention. There's a lesson there."* —**Mandy Hale**

**On my journey of self-development**, I ran across a video entitled, "The Game of Life and How to Play It", by Florence Scovel Shinn. A co-worker had given me a copy of a book with this same title about 30 years ago. I got up and walked over to my filing cabinet and found the book still there where I had filed it away. I do not know why I never gave it away or how I had managed to not carelessly misplace it. Something within me knew my path would lead me back to it. Somehow, I subconsciously knew the importance of the words this book contained.

*The Game of Life and How to Play It* was published in 1925. Shinn teaches in this book her philosophies based on the Laws of Metaphysics. Shinn writes about "The Law of Expectancy", where she emphasizes the power of the imagination to bring about life events. "Whatever man feels deeply or images clearly, is impressed upon the subconscious mind and carried out in minutest detail." Shinn also writes about, "The Devine Pattern of Intuition" and "The Law of Substitution" where, according to her, sometimes our desires are misdirected. "Many people are in ignorance of their true destinies and are striving for things and situations which do not belong to them and would only bring failure and dissatisfaction if attained." Shinn also covers the "Law of Non-Resistance", "The Law of Forgiveness", "The Law of Use" and "The Law of Love" in her book. The book is a treasure, filled with value for your life's journey.

One excerpt from Shinn's book reads, "Many people do not receive their heart's desire because they desire it too intensely. They are longing for it instead of feeling they have already received it. If you believed that before you called, you were answered, then you would be quite free from worry and anxiety, and live joyfully in the moment. When you can be happy with or without your heart's desire, it will suddenly appear, for your ship will come in over a 'don't care' sea. Be happy and something will happen. Feel rich, and riches will manifest on the external."

Shinn goes on to say, "All suffering is a spiritual alarm clock. You have been asleep about something. Perhaps you have been unjust, unforgiving, ungrateful, critical, or intolerant. Perhaps you were afraid to follow an intuitive lead. Suddenly the karmic factories begin working, for the 'way of the transgressor is hard. I call on the law of forgiveness. I am free from mistakes. I am under grace and not under karmic law."

I remember reading some of the content when my coworker gave it to me, but I guess I was too young, or rather not in alignment with myself enough, to know the value of what had been given to me at the age of 20, so I didn't read the entire book.

I sat there and listened to the video. The words were so powerful that I could not stop listening. I found myself constantly rewinding to get clarification and understanding about the game of life and how to play it. It's amazing how things come full circle for us when it is meant for us to have as a piece of the puzzle that completes our life.

Now, I could understand the message, the meaning behind the spoken words. Shinn spoke of forgiving the person(s) who have harmed you by sending them love and goodwill, saying, "I forgive them." Shinn says that, "like a kaleidoscope, the whole situation changes, for love is the fulfillment of the law. Your seeming enemies are transmuted into friends and, consciously or unconsciously, serve the Divine Plan of your life."

Shinn explains that you must answer each negative thought with a word of authority because if you entertain them or give them attention, it will encamp in your consciousness. Your doubts and fears and resentment will settle down to result in a harvest of misfortune. "Every great work, every big accomplishment, has been brought into manifestation through holding to the vision, and often just before the big achievement, comes apparent failure and discouragement. When man can wish without worrying, every desire will be instantly fulfilled." Florence Scovel Shinn.

I was listening to comedian Steve Harvey on YouTube as he quoted scripture from James 4:2 (KJV Bible). He said, "We have not because we ask not." Steve went on to say, "Write the vision and make it plain", from Habakkuk 2 (KJV Bible). He meant the visions that come to us through our imaginations. Only we can see our imaginations, only we know the things that will bring us true fulfillment. This is why, when I asked others what they thought about me enrolling in Les Brown's Academy, they could not see the value. As Steve Harvey said in the video, "God did not put it in their head, he put it in my head." I now realize that they could not see it because the vision was not given to *them*, it was given to *me*. Remember, other people cannot see the things you imagine or envision and may not understand the significance.

Many people do not understand the priceless act of writing their vision down. We must take responsibility for seeing our visions through and doing what it takes to arrive at our destiny. You have to get it out of your head and onto paper.

I enjoy sitting alone in a quiet space. There is something about the silence and stillness that sparks my imagination to reveal the action steps needed to connect my vision to purpose. I was sitting and thinking one day about how many years people waste just drifting through life, not knowing how to find their true purpose, how to find themselves, or how to free themselves of all the fear we face over and over again.

I believe that it is not until we understand how the mind works that we can begin to move forward toward true success, true abundance, and true joy. It is critical that we understand that it does not just happen to other people. It is within our reach; we have to take the time to go get it and believe that it is possible for us to have, if only we embrace our abilities and ourselves.

Today, I say to you, stop doubting yourself. Speak up and live your life to the fullest. Stop holding back and wondering what others will think of you. Who cares? It is your time to love yourself, be yourself and live your dreams.

When you think of your success, what does that look like for you? Is it attaining a certain income, a certain position, or achieving great experiences with family?

What does it look like? Only you know. Now, think of how to position yourself on the path to self-discovery, self-improvement, and fulfillment. On your journey to success, it will not always be smooth and challenge-free. It is critical that we are able to understand that each challenge along the way will make us stronger, better, and more resilient.

Sometimes, things will come full circle, like the book I found years later by Florence Scovel Shinn. Remember that when they do, take advantage of the opportunity and seek to find the relevance. It just might be a missing piece that leads you to your dream.

We must always learn from each experience as we get closer and closer to our goal, our success. This is no different from learning to ride a bike. You kept falling but you kept getting back up and getting back on the bike until you learned how to ride. I remember falling in a sticker bush when I first started riding my bike. I was embarrassed, hurt and scratched all up, but I got up, dusted myself off, picked up my bike out of the sticker bush, got back on and started riding again. Life is no different. We will succeed if we do not stop. We can't allow the challenges we face to stop us. You have to want to succeed just as badly as you wanted to learn to ride the bike. You must have the *never give up, never quit* attitude. We must learn the value of becoming our own best fan and how to motivate ourselves when times get difficult.

We will become discouraged sometimes, of course, but our reason for achieving our goal and our ability to self-motivate will keep us pushing forward. You are worthy of your goals, just as much as anyone else. What God does for others he will also do for you. Don't get caught up blaming others and feeling jealous of others because you feel they are where you want to be, or feel they are in the way of you achieving your goals and dreams. When we do this, we lose focus; we are not trusting our higher power or our abilities. You have what it takes, focus only on you, and do not compare yourself to others and their progress. Do not allow others to make you doubt your gifts and abilities.

I remember growing up as a child, with no thoughts other than observing the beauty of time; where I existed. I knew who I was in that space, at that time. I would lie in bed at night and dream of the person I wanted to become as an adult. I remember looking in big catalog books that were given out in stores and also sent to homes of customers. I can still remember the smile on my face and the joy in my heart as my friends and I would go through each page pointing and marking what we would have in our homes when we grew up. We dreamed of the perfect husband and children, the perfect family. Our dreams kept us excited and anxious about our perfect future so full of love, excitement, and enjoyment. Then life began to hit us, one at a time. We each went through our unique experiences of joy and pain. Our belief in ourselves began to change and fade. Sometimes, people, places and environments can take us so far off our path to greatness that it becomes difficult to find our way back.

I think what makes it so difficult is that we do not understand the process, we think from the outside in, because we have not learned how to handle the challenges of life, so we become stuck in the moment. We let the things going on around us dictate our actions instead of tapping into our true power, the power within us, to dictate how we react to the things going on outside of us. We have the mental capacity to stay in control of our actions. We just have to use the power we have. We have to pause and think things through, and then react.

Learning how to deal with situations comes after dealing with several challenges and overcoming them; developing resilience and getting back on track. Many of us just do not know how to use the power of our mind (think from the inside out) and not let our circumstances change who we are.

It is because we have not learned how to use our minds that we allow ourselves to become absorbed in fear, pain, and heartache. We shut ourselves off, become distant, depressed and withdrawn. We stop dreaming; stop doing the things that make us happy; we stop being true to ourselves.

I think we really have to look at the choices we make and ask, do they make us better or bitter? Do they add positivity and value to your life or negativity and self-doubt?

We should never change ourselves to fit in, or to make someone love us. There is a saying, "Be yourself or be by yourself". A person can only pretend for so long, and then the real person will resurface. If someone truly loves you for you, it frees you from pretending to be someone you are not. To be happy, you have to be you.

We have to love ourselves enough to stay true to who we are. We have to grow and become one with our true purpose. Ask yourself, what do you want? Bob Proctor said, "Thoughts become things, if you see it in your mind, you can hold it in your hand." Les Brown said, "You have to take responsibility for your own life, to have the things you want, only you can do that."

So, as you sit there, in your quiet space, close your eyes and relax. Start to think about what will bring you the most fulfillment and joy in your life. You only get one life and there is only one you. You owe it to yourself to live a life full of purpose, excitement, and happiness. Make a commitment today to not allow others to steal that from you. It is not only important, but also necessary for you to do that.

I heard the comedian Katt Williams say, "You have to stay in tune with your star player" which is you. You have to know who you are. You have to know what your purpose is for being on this earth.

When you get to the end of your journey through life, what will you say about the life you lived? The time to align yourself and your actions toward those things is now, so that you can smile and say, "I have no regrets, I lived a life that I am so proud of." Finding this book so many years later was the piece I needed to support my journey to greatness. It reinforced the power of positive thinking, love and forgiveness. Listening to the audiobook grabbed me and redirected my thoughts. I said to myself; *You need to take a look at the power of your mind more seriously. Be mindful of the thoughts you entertain, the thoughts you give time and energy to.* I am reminded of James Allen when he said, "A man is literally what he thinks, his character being the complete sum of all his thoughts."

Remember, when life brings you full circle, pause and ask yourself, why am I seeing this again? As Mandy Hale said, "There's a lesson there."

# Florence Scovel Shinn

## Affirmations for Forgiveness

"I forgive everyone and everyone forgives me. The gates swing open for my good.

I call on the law of forgiveness. I am free from mistakes and the consequences of mistakes. I am under grace and not under karmic law.

Though my mistakes be as scarlet, I shall be washed whiter than snow.

What didn't happen in the Kingdom never happened anywhere."

**—Florence Scovel Shinn**

CHAPTER FIVE

# Believing in Yourself

*"God doesn't do the work for you; he does the work through you. It's not enough to look up; you must also look within."*
—Patti LaBelle.

**Time to start believing in yourself.** Many people struggle with just knowing how to believe in themselves. First, you have to be willing to take a chance on your dreams. You have to believe in yourself enough to know that it is possible you can live your dream.

Regardless of the circumstances, we find ourselves in, we must always look for the lesson, pick ourselves up and keep it moving. Take the time to analyze the issue, understand the root cause, and correct it. Don't dwell on it. Use it as fuel to become better.

Think of what is stopping you from achieving your goals and dreams. Is it one of the things on your fear list? Do you feel scared or uncertain? What do you do in those moments of doubt and confusion? Whenever I am feeling scared or uncertain, I pause for a moment, close my eyes, and think of my favorite memory of my father, the late John D Brown. The thoughts are so clear and vivid that I can remember them as though the events happened yesterday.

I see myself sitting across the table from him. I hear his voice saying, "It is time for you to make your move, stay calm, stay focused, read the board and make your move. You can do this." I sit and think about it, looking at my situation and my options for beating him in a game of checkers. What do I do next? What is my next move?

All of this, I remember from sitting across the table from him, strategizing for the win. I am not sure if you are familiar with this game, but the encyclopedia Britannica describes it as "also being called draughts, which is a board game, one of the world's oldest games. Checkers is played by two persons who oppose each other across a board of 64 light and dark squares, the same as a chessboard. There are 24 playing pieces which are disk shaped and of contrasting colors. A win is scored when an opponent's pieces are all captured or blocked so that they cannot move." My family and I enjoyed this game as a pastime because my father, who was very good at it, introduced it to us. My dad believed that many values and lessons could be learned through this game; lessons that we would take into our adulthood.

The game is simple but poses many mental challenges. Skills such as patience, resiliency, strategizing and seeing opportunities can all be demonstrated through this game. This is what my father meant when he said, "Read the board." He meant, to look at the position of every checker on the checkerboard before you make your move because your opponent may be setting you up for a trap. This is also true in life, everything I learned in that game, I have found to be beneficial, as I have dealt with challenges, wins and losses in life. All learned through a fun, yet simple, game.

Humans have the tendency to dream and envision; envision abundance, perhaps. Then the negative commentary begins to appear in our minds. In addition, we start to doubt ourselves. We start to doubt all the dreams that we have, we start to doubt our ability to have the things that we have wanted for so long. Most of us find ourselves in "fight or flight" mode. We stop. We become stuck; we park and sometimes get comfortable sitting in the same spot. You know, some of us even blame our circumstances for where we are — "If only I were richer, smarter, better looking" — but I take George Bernard Shaw's approach and I do not believe in circumstances. He said that the people who succeed in this life are the people who look for the circumstances they want, and if they cannot find them, they create them. So, I say to you, stop blaming your circumstances. Ask yourself: *Am I able? In addition, am I willing? If I am able, am I willing to do whatever is required of me to live out my goals, my dream, and my destiny?*

There was a time in my life when I felt sad, I felt lost, and I felt so confused. I remember sitting in a room, in a chair in front of a TV that was turned off. I can remember just staring; my heart was beating so slowly, and it felt so heavy. My mind was so full of regret, guilt, and shame for being in the place I was in, making the mistakes I had made. I could see no direction for my life. I was filled with fear. In addition, I thought, *Do I have what it takes to move forward? Do I have what it takes for me to succeed in life?*

I closed my eyes, and the memory of my father appeared: "You can do this." No matter where you are stuck in life right now, it is time for you to make your next move. You can do this. If you put your mind to it, you will do it. Being stuck is part of the human experience. It is normal to be stuck in the moment, thinking about all the things that have happened, thinking about our fears, But Zig Ziglar once famously said, "Fear has two meanings: Forget everything and run or face everything and rise." Which will you choose? What are you going to do with all your goals and your dreams, your destiny? Whatever your fears are, I want you to face them, and I want you to say, "I can do this! I can overcome the fear and I can keep moving in the direction of my dream."

Henry Ford reminded us of this when he said, "One of the greatest discoveries a man can make is one of his great surprises." That is, conquering our fear when we did not believe we could. After all, what stops you is simply your unwillingness to go through it.

I want to share five powerful Cs with you. The first one is *clarity*. I want you to have a clear mental vision of your true purpose. This is necessary to begin your journey. I want you to have *confidence*, by reminding yourself of your achievements each day and at least five things you are grateful for; this is the second C. The third C is for *commitment*; not only to the tasks ahead of you, but also to yourself. The fourth C is for *challenging*. You must continue to challenge yourself and push through all the negativity and the adversity. Finally, the last C, is for *courage*. Have the courage to win and to live out your true purpose, you owe that to yourself.

Let the words of Nelson Mandela echo through your life, "I learned that courage was not the absence of fear, but the triumph over it." He said that the brave man is not he who does not feel afraid, but he who conquers that fear. Therefore, it is time for you to say, "I can do this; I can conquer the fear that is holding me back."

I want you to look at your goals and your dreams today. Look at where you are and question it. Are you where you want to be at this time in your life? Is there more for you?

A lot of us try to look at the big picture and that is important. Nevertheless, Robert Shuler Smith believes, as do I, that "by the yard it's hard, but inch by inch it's a cinch." So, take it step by step if you must, and just keep moving until you achieve your goals, your dreams and eventually your destiny.

Do not just drift through life, take the time to live a life of impact and value, live a life that will outlive you. Myles Monroe, a Bahamian Christian evangelist, ordained Pentecostal minister, public speaker and author said, "If you want to become successful, seek to become a person of value." He said, "The value of life is not in its duration, but in its donation. You are not important because of how long you live; you are important because of how effective you live. And most people are concerned about growing old rather than being effective." He said, "Your value in life is determined by the problems you solve through your gift."

Every time I close my eyes, I see my father, I hear his voice and I feel his presence. He has become my mantra, my way of moving forward. When you close your eyes what do you see?

"Vision is the Source and hope of life. The greatest gift ever given to mankind is not the gift of sight, but the gift of vision. Sight is a function of the eyes; vision is a function of the heart. 'Eyes that look are common, but eyes that see are rare.' Nothing noble or noteworthy on earth was ever done without vision."

—**Myles Munroe**

CHAPTER SIX

# Develop your Mind for Greatness.

*"Lost time is never found again."* —Benjamin Franklin

**What are you doing with your time?** It is so easy to waste your time and allow others to use it up. Again, I ask you, what are you doing with your time? It is important for you to know how it is spent.

My mom often would say, as I was growing up, "People will spend your time like they spend your money and people will use you like they use toothpaste and soap" if you allow them.

I remember losing my money as a child. I had gotten a dollar that I had earned from doing chores. I asked my mom if I could go to the neighborhood store, which was in walking distance. She said yes; I was so happy to go spend the dollar. I remember getting to the store and I did not have the dollar. I searched everywhere; I could not find it. I panicked; I began searching in my pockets, all around me and on the ground. I realized I must have lost it on my way to the store. I tried to backtrack my route to see if I could find it. I could not; I did not see it anywhere. My heart just sank. I felt sad and defeated after searching for so long. Some people may say, "Really, over a dollar?" As a child however, that loss was significant to me. I went to my father and told him I had lost my dollar going to the store. My dad said, don't worry over it. He said, "Whoever found that dollar must have needed it more than you did. God will bless you with more." As a child, I did not understand. I still cried, but I took my dad's word for it and went on about my day.

There was a grocery store where we often shopped not far from where we lived. The store gave out game cards with store purchases. The game cards came with little numbered paper chips. You had to match the number on each chip to the number on the card, like the game bingo. We went to the store a few days after I had lost my dollar. After buying groceries, the clerk gave my parents a hand full of chips, along with a game card. My parents gave them to me because they knew I liked matching the chips to the numbers on the cards. I sat in the back seat of our car, while my father drove us home, matching the chips to the numbers. After placing the chips on the card, I realized that I had all chips for the 300-dollar prize. I told my parents and they said "Really?" I could tell they thought maybe I had placed one of the chips in the wrong place. I was only about 8 years old at the time. Once we got home, my parents reviewed my card and the chip placement and they realized that I had been correct. My parents drove back to the store and showed the store manager the card and sure enough, I had won 300 dollars. Immediately my dad's words came to mind about the dollar I had lost. Even though my father is no longer living, I took that lesson into my adult years. Whenever I lost something, I knew my blessings would continue to come, so even though I would initially get frustrated, a sigh of relief would come over me as my father's words came to mind. The dollar would then flash in my mind. I would smile and say, "Really, over a dollar Shirley?" It wasn't about the dollar, but the lesson that was invaluable. The memory of that moment makes me smile every time I think of it.

It is amazing how we can turn bad situations into better situations if we look at it from a positive point of view. Losing that dollar was a valuable lesson for me. The mere thought of it has gotten me through some difficult times throughout my journey through life. I learned not to waste my time on the small things that happen in life. I save my energy to get through the big challenges. I know going through challenges is a part of my growth process and is necessary in order to live a life that will not only serve me but also serve others, well. I still get knocked down by some challenges, however, I get up more quickly now. Experience has been a great teacher. Myles Monroe said, "We are a sum total of what we have learned from all who have taught us, both great and small."

Therefore, a lot of the problems we face are a result of learned behaviors. Think about it for a moment. What belief system have you developed over time? What ideas have you bought into that are not benefiting you? This is why, when we are trying to change our behavior, we have to look not only at ourselves but also our environment and the people we interact with.

To change our behavior, we have to take the time to develop our minds. Never be afraid to ask for help along your journey through life. My mentor Les Brown says, "Ask for help not because you are weak. But because you want to remain strong." Do not fret over your losses in life; shift your focus to the gains. Remember, they both shape us to become unique beings. Use your time and mind to propel yourself to abundance of happiness, wealth, joy, and peace. Do not allow others to waste your time; do not allow others to waste your mental space by dwelling on their selfish acts.

Know that if only you believe, no one can stop you from getting what is yours by divine right. In addition, if you lose something along the way, know that it was meant for another person on their journey to greatness and God has something else for you. So, keep your eyes open so you do not miss it when it comes to you. Remember that the things we need do not always come in the package we expect. Always search deeper than the surface and find the true value of a man or woman and the true value in the situation. It is there; we just have to look for it.

Are you allowing fear to stop you from pursuing that which you desire? Sometimes you simply have to sit still long enough to see it; to realize what you are seeking is also seeking you and is right within your grasp. Keep your eyes open so you don't miss your opportunity.

CHAPTER SEVEN

# Time to Act

*"Don't allow your past or present condition to control you. It's just a process that you're going through to get you to the next level."*
—TD Jakes

**Time to act.** As I sit here typing, I am thinking of all the time I have spent in my life trying to be the best version of myself; trying to find out what my unique talent, my unique gift is, and my divine purpose.

Can you imagine for a moment, having the ability to travel back in time and being able to right the wrongs we have done to others and right the wrongs which were done to us? Wouldn't that fix so many of the problems we have been holding on to for so many years? On the other hand, would it be as we have seen in the movies where when the past was altered, new problems were created? We do not get to meet the special persons we have grown to cherish; we miss some of the special places we had the opportunity to go to and experience. So, when we look at it from this perspective, we have to begin to focus on all those things, good and bad, that helped shape us into the wonderful person we've become.

As I sit here today, I cannot help but wonder how I ended up here. Let's go back about 37 years. I had just graduated from Forest Hill High School in Jackson, MS. I was so excited to be headed to college and majoring in nursing. I remember touring Tuskegee University and considering their Nursing program after I finished Jackson State University's Biology Pre-Nursing program. After finishing the pre-nursing program, I decided to change my major to Social Work. I remember working full-time and going to school full-time. It is amazing how life has a way of putting us on a completely different path from the one we had chosen. Think for a moment of where you are today. Are you where you intended to be? Are you living the life you dreamed about as a child; the perfect life? What happened to those dreams? Life has a way of putting us on so many different paths. We can become so lost and find ourselves so far off course from our dream, our vision of true abundance and happiness. Joel Osteen said, "Don't worry about your future or how you're going to accomplish a dream. God has already lined up what you need." I paused and asked God for guidance, and then I knew I had to pay close attention so I would not miss my blessing, my truly divine path. I knew I had allowed others to plant seeds of becoming a nurse in my head. I had wandered down a path others had chosen for me. I wasted so much time.

I remember going to work every day at a manufacturing plant. This was a chapter in my life that would connect me to my true purpose. However, at the time, I merely saw it as a means of survival. I was so young. I met three older women there who took me under their wings. I know now that they were placed there by God to guide me. Their names were Mrs. Dorothy, Ms. Wiliette and Mrs. Maggie. I would sit with them every day for lunch and listen to their conversation and guidance. One day I was working, and I noticed one of the Plant Managers, Robert, standing in front of a door, which led to the office area where the Supervisors and top management sat. I continued working as though I did not see him. The line I worked on just happened to be right in front of this entrance. I now know that this was not by chance, but God had placed me there. Later that day, I was asked to follow my supervisor and he led me through the door where I had seen Robert earlier that day. Through that door, there was a hallway, which led to a large office. When I entered the office, I noticed Robert sitting at a desk. My manager left after taking me there. I was offered a seat. Robert said he had heard I had been working full time for three years and going to school full time and was about to graduate. He asked me how long before I graduated. I explained that I had in fact been working and going to school full time and would be graduating in a couple of weeks. He said that he had noticed my work ethic and would like to offer me a position as a supervisor, if I was interested. He explained that the company had, up until about a month ago, only had males in the supervisory roles. They had hired one female, but she only stayed one week and quit. He asked how I felt about the position. I explained that I had only seen men in that role, but I felt like it was something I could do. My life had been very difficult; I thought to myself, this job could not be as difficult as what I had been going through. Robert did not know that I had just gotten up off my knees, praying for a blessing. I had just prayed and asked God to please put the right people in my path to guide me. Life was hard after my dad died in 1982. I often felt like it was me against the World and quitting was not an option. Could I handle it? I smiled inside because I knew who had sent this man to me. I had gotten to the end of my rope, so to speak. My car had broken down about two months before I graduated. I remember spending all the money I had worked for to pay taxicabs to take me to school and to my internship and I had to pay someone to take me to work. I felt defeated. I got on my knees that morning because I felt I had pushed myself to my limit. I asked God for help. I have often heard people say that there is something about stillness and prayer. Things really do happen. Sometimes, when we have done all that we feel that we can do and we have taken as much as we can stand, we have to kneel and pray.

I was in a store one day recently and passed by a plaque on a shelf that read, "When you have taken more than you can stand, kneel." Those words brought tears to my eyes as I thought about my past and the moments I had done just as the plaque read. I remember going into the restroom after I left Robert's office, I just could not believe how fast God worked for me that day. I knew it had to be God telling me not to worry because he had me. Again, this reminds me of Joel Osteen when he said, "Don't worry about your future or how you're going to accomplish a dream. God has already lined up what you need." This win was my sign to keep moving toward my dream. I graduated and accepted the offer and was promoted to Supervisor. I was the only female Manufacturing Production Supervisor for many years at that location.

I remember my first day, being introduced to the men at this big table where they sat and talked, man talk, during their breaks. I remember walking into the office during my break and I could hear them talking loudly until I entered the room. Once they saw my face, complete silence filled the air. This went on for a couple of weeks. One day while sitting there, one of the men said, " Look, I cannot take this. This is the rule of the office. What goes on in here stays in here." I said, "I am okay with that." The men became more comfortable with my presence and started talking more and more as time progressed. One day we had a new male supervisor start. I walked into the office to take a break and he stopped talking when I entered the office break room. The male supervisors asked him why he stopped talking. He said, "She just came in." They said, "Who, Brown? Oh, she is one of us. She doesn't care about what you are talking about. Besides, we tested her several times when she started. She is not the gossiping type." They all started laughing and someone said, "Isn't that right Brown?" I said, "What did you say?" They laughed and said, "We told you."

Calmness of mind, hard work, trust, and respect helped me develop a bond with this group of male supervisors and managers that I will cherish for a lifetime. I disrupted their state of equilibrium, their balance, but I knew that I belonged there. Although coworkers, they treated me as an equal business partner and the sister that most of them did not have. I smile thinking about how God placed them in my path to greatness. Remember that situations don't always start out smooth or without challenges, but in time, can develop into a treasure of a lifetime. It is how you see the situations you find yourself in. Look for the good in each encounter and always carry your own weight. Seek to add value to the team or situation.

That is how I got off the Nursing path to Social Work and then to Manufacturing Supervisor. I learned so many lessons during this time in my life and met so many wonderful people. I found that when you surround yourself with quality people, they truly do lift you up, which gives you the energy and desire that is needed to keep going after your dreams. Quality people say things to inspire and fuel your dreams because they want you to succeed. They want you to grow beyond your current circumstances.

James Allen said, "Calmness of mind is one of the beautiful jewels of wisdom. It is the result of long and patient effort in self-control. Its presence is an indication of ripened experience, and of a more than ordinary knowledge of the laws and operations of thought."

I am reminded of Myles Munroe when he said, **"If you want to become successful, seek to become a person of value."**

CHAPTER EIGHT

# Shift your Mindset

*"Change the way you look at things and the things you look at change."* —Wayne W. Dyer

Shift your Mindset. We all want to know the steps needed to get where we want to be in life. But many just don't know how to shift their mindset to create the change they desire. We have the power and ability to change our thoughts and beliefs. The power lies in understanding how our thoughts lead to our outcomes.

You will bring into your life more power, more wealth, more health, more happiness, and more delight by learning to associate and discharge the control of your subconscious mind. You need not obtain this power; you already have it. But, you need to learn how to utilize it; you need to get it so that you simply can apply it inside all divisions of your life. Within the depths of your subconscious lies infinite wisdom, infinite power, and an infinite supply of all that is essential for development and expression. Start today to recognize these possibilities of your mind and they will take shape within the world.

Remember, it is our thoughts that create our feelings. It is our feelings that create the actions, and it is through our actions that we achieve the results that we seek. So, in essence, how we think influences how we feel and how we feel influences our behavior and how we behave influences how we live our lives and the choices we make. There are consequences we live with as a result of events and our beliefs. However, we can change how we internalize the events we encounter. We can learn how to shift our unhelpful thought process to a helpful thought process. We have the power and mental ability to access our inner conversations and reflect on them. Our beliefs have highly personal meanings to us. We have to understand what our beliefs mean to us.

Once we identify what is causing unwanted results in our lives, we can take steps to change our circumstances. Try using these five steps to change.

Acknowledging that you are responsible for creating your own emotional problems

1. Accepting you that you have the ability to change disturbances significantly

2. Recognizing emotional problems stem from irrational beliefs

3. Seeing the value of disputing self-defeating beliefs

4. Accepting the fact that in order to change, we must work hard in emotional and behavioral ways to counteract irrational beliefs and dysfunctional feelings and behaviors.

Our irrational ideas lead to self-defeating behavior. For example, we may find ourselves thinking that we must have love and approval from everyone we surround ourselves with. This is irrational thinking. We change our beliefs by disputing our irrational thinking, we have to practice a new thought process and validate our thoughts against evidence. The key is, the more you practice the better you will become.

Some techniques that will help include talking to others who are going through the same fears, researching your issues/fears to get a better understanding, being open-minded and motivated to change, and being willing to take a deep look at your fears to determine if they are rational or irrational. Expect to endure moments of emotional discomfort during your transition through the development process. Remember, you are challenging your beliefs, which are often beliefs we have had for a long time.

Learning how to change our thoughts and beliefs is the key to getting the results we want. Our brain has the ability to change and reorganize itself based on changes in our environment, thoughts, emotions, and behavior. We can train our brains through repetition and practice to think and function differently.

We are able to change, over time, by thinking differently and by creating positive feelings and actions to counteract the feelings, thoughts and actions that are not serving us well. Over time, our brains forget the old beliefs and create new beliefs.

Often, when we go after our dreams, we allow fear to stop us. Fear limits our potential for success because our fear and anxiety don't allow us to move past that which we have developed a fear or phobia of. It creates a gap between where we are and where we want to be in life. It is stopping you from realizing your goals and dreams. Keep in mind that if we have a fear of something, our lives are limited by that fear. However, fear is a normal part of our thinking process. Fear is a function of the cerebellum, which is the part of the brain that is responsible for the fight, flight, or freeze response. Its function is to keep us safe. It is important that we recognize this function because when we decide to go after our dreams, we will have feelings of fear. You can't let it stop you. Recognize you are feeling fear because you are trying to do something you have never done before, your cerebellum is telling you that it is unsafe, you become fearful and doubtful and will often see it as a sign to stop. Don't stop. You now understand that it is merely how the brain is supposed to work. Push through your fears and go after the change you seek.

There is power in our thoughts. Once we learn how to manage our minds, we can change the way we feel by changing our thoughts. You have the power to dictate how you think, feel, and act. We can create the life we seek; we don't have to blame our circumstances for where we are in life.

In order to truly achieve great success, whatever that means to you, you will need to shift your mindset so that your beliefs and actions are aligned with what you really want. Remember that our mindset is made up of a set of beliefs that have been shaped by our past experiences, our environment, and our interactions. Our mindset can stop us from achieving our goals in life and living the life we deserve. But we can change our thoughts by shifting and reshaping them to become more productive by identifying the beliefs that are holding us back. Write them down. Begin changing the limiting beliefs you identify. Be mindful that your brain, out of fear, will give you all kinds of reasons why you should not or cannot achieve what you are trying to accomplish. Recognize that you are in your comfort zone, but once you realize that there is no growth there, you must move; push through your fear and doubt. Commit to yourself that you will stop making excuses for failed goals. Own up to it and plan to arrive at your goals and dreams.

Your confidence will develop as you begin to act. As your confidence level increases, so too will your momentum, propelling you toward what you thought, at one time, was impossible. You have arrived. You just had to believe in yourself and act toward your dream.

Changing your mindset starts with believing in yourself, and reminding yourself daily of how great you are. Empower yourself to change and make better choices, you have to believe that what you want is possible for you to have, remind yourself to look for the good in every situation instead of dwelling on the bad. Love yourself enough to be your own unique self, leave the doubt and fear behind. Remember to be grateful for what you do have and live in the moment. Commit to appreciating the journey to your life of abundance and happiness.

You have the power within you to change your mindset so you can change your life. Find what works best for you and stick to that. I am reminded of a quote I read from an anonymous author, it read, "Whatever you hold in your mind will tend to occur in your life. If you continue to believe as you have always believed, you will continue to act as you have always acted. If you continue to act as you have always acted, you will continue to get what you have always gotten. If you want different results in your life or your work, **all you have to do is change your mind**." You have the power to succeed and live an abundant life.

You have a mind, and you should learn how to use it. The main point to remember is once the subconscious mind accepts an idea, it begins to execute it. However, when your habitual thinking is harmonious and constructive, you experience perfect health, success, and prosperity.

Peace of mind and a healthy body are inevitable when you begin to think and feel in the right way. The only thing required for you to do is to get your conscious mind to accept your idea, and the law of your own subconscious mind will bring forth the health, peace, or position you desire. The law of your mind is this: you will get a reaction or response from your subconscious mind according to the nature of the thought or idea you hold in your conscious mind.

Begin today sowing thoughts of peace, joy, right action and success. Think discreetly and with intrigued interest about these qualities and acknowledge them completely in your conscious reasoning mind. Proceed to plant these brilliant seeds (thoughts) within your mind and you will reap a brilliant harvest. Your subconscious mind can develop all sorts of seeds, good or bad. Each thought is, therefore, a cause, and each condition is an effect. For this reason, it is fundamental that you simply take charge of your thoughts so as to bring forth only desirable outcomes.

CHAPTER NINE

# Finding your Divine Purpose, your Gift

*"If you cannot figure out your purpose, figure out your passion. For your passion will lead you right into your purpose."* —TD Jakes

**Divine Purpose.** As I sit here alone, I am thinking about how many years we waste just drifting through life, not knowing how to find our true purpose, how to find ourselves and how to free ourselves from all the fear we face over and over again. It is not until we understand how the mind works that we can begin to move forward toward true success, true abundance, and true joy.

We all deserve to live the life we dream about. It is when we open our mind and heighten our awareness of self that we begin to see that abundance does not just happen to other people. It is within our reach if only we take the time to go get it. Yes, it is possible for us to have, if only we believe in our abilities and ourselves.

Life does not always run smoothly for any of us and many steps taken with the best intentions in the world do not always turn out as well as expected.

Even under ideal conditions, we are faced with problems day after day, which call for us to make specific decisions. Some decisions involve only minor adjustments; others require drastic changes or complete reversals in habitual behavior. But whatever the need, our feelings or emotions in the moment influence our actions and greatly affect our final decisions. To be able to meet conditions as they arise you have to be prepared for them. However, unfortunately, many individuals are disadvantaged from the start. Whether due to environment, personal make-up, conditioned reflexes, preconceived notions, lack of self-reliance, or emotional instability, many of us have a hard time facing realistically the everyday problems of life. We look for a way out and seek to escape imminent changes or new responsibilities. We try to ignore them, to immerse or suppress them, and that often marks the beginning of a complex or a neurosis.

The driving force for most of us is the need to feel respected and appreciated. Janet Jackson said it was her belief that, "We all have the need to feel special. In addition, this need can bring out the best in us, yet the worst in us." We must be mindful of how we react to all people and all situations. In spite of challenges and controversy, don't spend time doubting yourself. Speak up when needed and appreciate your journey. Move past wondering what others think of you. You don't need their approval when you are in alignment with your purpose. Believe me, the people around you can't help but take notice.

A coworker of mine was fired from her job. People were asking her what she was going to do. She replied, "God has something better for me." I smiled and again thought about my lost dollar. I thought, *She is so right.* I believe that sometimes, when God wants us to do something that aligns with our divine purpose, he will alter our path to get us to go in the right direction.

I have found comfort in searching within myself to find out why my life is going a certain way, and dissecting my emotions at times of confusion and uncertainty. Why am I being faced with so much adversity, so many obstacles, why, why, why? I too, just like the former coworker, pray for clarity and guidance. I find comfort in this because I know that once the storm of life is over, I will be a better, stronger, unique being. I know that with each storm, I grow and become a much larger version and expression of myself. With each storm, I grow to know myself more and more. With each storm, I learn to appreciate the sunny days, the calm days, the quiet moments, joy, and peace of mind.

I used to find myself sleeping to pass the time. It just felt like when I was asleep, I could not think about the pain I was feeling. I knew it could only heal with time. But the thing about sleeping the pain away is that when you awaken, the pain is still there, waiting for you. Sometimes, it will wake you up out of your sleep. Moreover, I found that when dealing with the struggles of life, time seems to pass so slowly.

I have come to realize that in every pain there is a lesson. You just have to make sure you learn the lesson so that you do not have to keep going through storms for the same lesson. I heard a man say once "Some people are so closed-minded, you can try to warn them about danger in life and they still won't listen." He said, "You can tell that person that if they go to the end of the street, do not turn left because there is a huge hole there, if you turn left you will fall into the hole as soon as you turn and I bet you, someone will walk to the end of the street, turn left, and fall in the hole." Some people are just that way. So, do not be that way. Always listen and have an open mind. Take your time to figure out the lesson to be learned in each storm you go through in life. Listen to the people you trust and respect and don't be afraid to ask for help when you get off track.

Winston Churchill said, "Courage is what it takes to stand up and speak; courage is also what it takes to sit down and listen." This statement is very powerful. Now, with that being said, let's get started on aligning our vision to our purpose, identifying our power to succeed, and using it to redefine our journey to living a happy and successful life.

CHAPTER TEN

# Aligning Vision to Divine Purpose

*"Purpose is when you know and understand what you were born to accomplish. Vision is when you see it in your mind and begin to imagine it."* —**Myles Munroe**

**Aligning Vision to Purpose.** I remember running through the grass as a child and picking the dandelions and blowing the seeds into the wind and watching them float gently. I made small wishes as the seeds floated into the wind. As many people do, I believed that blowing the seeds away would bring good luck and my wishes would be granted. Memories like these always calm me and bring an innocent smile to my face.

We all have had visions and dreams of being more and doing more. Have you ever stopped to think about why you have not achieved your desired outcome? I challenge you to close your eyes and think for a moment…

Let's go back to the days when you walked into a room and the whole room seemed to light up with your presence because you brought such energy and glow with you. Remember the happiness and peace you felt in those moments. If only we knew how special those moments were and how much power we had. We were unstoppable.

I believe we all deserve that life of happiness. I was sitting and thinking about my age, my career and where I was in life at age 54. I had casually drifted through life and had ended up in good places, comfortable places. However, something was missing. I realized that I was settling for much less than I deserved. I had to figure it out quickly. I had to research and work to get myself on the right path to finding my true purpose. I had to stop and ask myself again what I truly wanted. What would make me happy? What was causing me to procrastinate when it came to my dreams and goals? How do I fix this? I had to admit that I did not know how.

It is amazing how much of a role our self-image plays in so many aspects of our lives. It can stop us from doing so much because our focus is on approval from others and being accepted and not on doing what we love to do.

What does it look like to be your true self? This is where you will find true happiness. People should accept and respect you for the unique gifts that you bring to the universe.

We were all born for something special, unique; something big. What is your special something? Think of your vision as your plan. We have to start with our vision. Without a goal, we find ourselves aimlessly drifting throughout life.

Surely, the thing that matters most in a man is the thing that is peculiar to him, his distinctive gift and aptitude, however small it may be. To realize that, fully develop it, and bring it to fruition is at once the full triumph of one's self and the supreme service one can render to mankind.

Therefore, what are the traits that will amplify and lead to your greatness? Moderation is important, however, pay attention to consistency; you should have courage, you need to improvise, you must save, you must read, and you need to speak and connect with the public. There are unpredictable errors that will detain or deter you and these have to be avoided. Although success brings power, only the proper use of power brings happiness. This is a sensible philosophy that has been handed down to generation after generation, many will find it useful, alternatively than inspirational, and for this materialistic world, realistic.

If you are still feeling confused and lost on your journey in life, I suggest finding a quiet place and being still. When you find your comfortable place, lie down, close your eyes, and relax. Some find that quiet music and meditation will help them gather their thoughts and determine their true purpose. It gives you the opportunity to focus without distractions.

We have to look beyond others who try to dim our light for their own selfish gain. Some will try to dim your light because they too would love to feel and glow as you do with an energy that is contagious. They are trying to figure out why you look so happy. What is causing the glow that comes into the room with you? They want what you have. They long for that place that you have found within yourself.

Visions are known to emerge from spiritual traditions and could provide a lens into human nature and reality. Prophecy is often associated with visions. The Merriam-Webster dictionary defines prophecy as "a statement, which predicts what is going to happen in the future, especially one that is based on what you or another believes about a particular matter, rather than existing facts."

Your visions, something you have seen in a dream, trance or ecstasy, a thought, concept, or object formed by your imagination, are personal and do not use the logical, thinking part of the mind.

I was sitting at my desk in 2003 when a woman named Kathy came to my office door. Kathy was excited and had a glow about her that immediately sparked a level of excitement in me. She asked if I was very busy and I replied "No, what do you have?" She said, "There is a woman who works here who has the gift of prophecy. Many people who have known her for years said that what she prophesies comes true." She said, "You should go out to the floor to see her." I said, "Girl, I am not sure if I want to know." Kathy continued to try to convince me to go to see the woman. A part of me wanted to go, but a part of me, fear, kept holding me back. I allowed my fear to override my desire to see this woman. I have often heard that what you seek is also seeking you. Days went by and I still had not gone out to see the woman.

I remember going to bed for nights wondering what this woman would tell me if I approached her. Then again, I was afraid of what she might say. One day, while sitting in my office, the Supervisor from the Production floor, Frank, came to my office. Frank asked me if I could help him with an issue he had in his area. I asked him what was going on. He mentioned that all the patties in his fryer were coming out curled up. By that point, I had forgotten about the prophet Kathy had told me about. I hurried out to the floor with Frank. Once I got there, I saw that the patties coming out of his fryer were curled up, just as he had described. I told him to lower the oil level in his fryer until the oil barely covered the top of the patties. Frank lowered the oil, and the patties began coming out straight and flat. He turned to me and said thank you. I stood there for a moment and watched him get his area straight after the issue was resolved.

While standing there, a woman approached me. She introduced herself and asked me if she could tell me something. I said, "Yes mam." She said, "You are not going to be at this company long. You will be offered another job opportunity and you will take it." She said, "It will be a good move for you, but before the end of your time, you will be speaking and spreading the word to thousands of people." I said "Really?" I thought: *This must be the woman Kathy had been trying to get me to speak to.* She came to me. It was as though she felt compelled to tell me what she had seen for me.

I went back to my office after speaking to her. I should have taken the time to ask her more about her vision, but fear stopped me again. I went on for years and years, wondering what she meant by saying I would be speaking to many people, spreading the word. What word? I initially thought that I would end up being an Evangelist and spreading the gospel. I asked a preacher if he could tell me what that meant, and he said it could mean many things. It could be spreading the gospel, but it could be spreading the word in a different way. I was lost. Well, in less than a year, I was offered a position at another company, and it did turn out to be a blessing for me, just as the nice older lady had prophesied.

I had my doubts initially, partly because I had been with the company for over 15 years. However, just as she said, I was offered the opportunity, I did take it, and just as she said, it proved to be a great opportunity for me.

I am still waiting to see how the second part of the prophecy will come about, but I have faith it too will show up in a powerful way and I will be spreading the word to many people. If you think about it, this book can be seen as a start to my spreading the word.

"We cannot always control our thoughts,
but we can control our words,
and repetition impresses the subconscious,
and we are then the master of the situation."
**—Florence Scovel Shinn**

CHAPTER ELEVEN

# Checking your Envy

*"What God does for others he does for me and more"*
—**Florence Scovel Shinn**

**Don't lose precious time envying others...** In Florence Scovel Shinn's book entitled *The Game of Life and How to Play It* she talks about being envious of others. We all have had thoughts of envy or jealousy surface at some point in our lives. I believe that this is common. However, I also believe that we must recognize those thoughts and feelings for what they are and call it out because it is wrong and can lead to self-destruction.

We should remind ourselves of what Florence mentions in her book, that what God does for others he will do for you. I have written her quote down in several places to remind myself. When an envious thought comes to my mind, I say to myself: *What God does for others he does for me and more.* This quote allows me to appreciate myself and give gratitude and sincere congratulations to those who deserve it because I understand that my time will come.

We all have our times of glory. We must understand that what is meant for us by Divine right, no one can take from us. You must believe this and not waste time being envious of anyone. Just the idea of thinking ill of someone else takes away precious time from attaining our dreams and goals. Believe me, it is not worth it. When these types of thoughts surface, push them out of your mind, shift your thoughts and do the right thing.

Give congratulations to others and keep moving toward your Divine blessings. You will meet them if you don't allow distractions such as envy and jealousy to stop you. You have the power to control your thoughts.

Florence Scovel Shinn says, "You can control any situation if you first control yourself." I challenge you today to stay in control of yourself in all situations. You must always expect the unexpected so that you will never be disappointed. Life will throw you curveballs, people will not always treat you the way they would want to be treated, and people who you felt you could trust will sometimes let you down. Just know this.

Also, remember that even you sometimes do not do what you thought you would do. Sometimes you also lie to yourself when you say you are not going to do something, but you do it anyway. We hold people to standards that we cannot even meet ourselves. So do not be too hard on yourself or others. Take one day at a time, one situation at a time and keep moving toward your goals and dreams.

Know that you will encounter setbacks but as Willie Jolley said, "A Setback is a Setup for a Comeback." Trust and believe that you have the power to bounce back and get back on your journey to greatness.

CHAPTER TWELVE

# Developing Calmness of Mind

*"The more tranquil a man becomes, the greater his success, his influence, his power for good. Calmness of mind is one of the beautiful jewels of wisdom. It is the result of long and patient effort in self-control. Its presence is an indication of ripened experience, and of a more than ordinary knowledge of the laws and operations of thought."* —**James Allen**

**Calmness of mind takes practice.** It takes practice not to be thrown off track. Learning how to stay focused amid challenges is a learned behavior. When you come to understand that challenges don't last always, and they too shall pass, you can begin to push through and keep moving toward your goals and dreams.

When I think of the idea of calmness of mind, I am reminded of Jules Renard when he said, "It doesn't pay to say too much when you are mad enough to choke. For the word that stings the deepest is the word that is never spoke. Let the other fellow wrangle till the storm has blown away, then he'll do a heap of thinking about the things you didn't say."

Each person must understand the value of knowing how to think into results. We have to learn how to control our thoughts and emotions. We all have visions but until you understand how to take those visions and turn them into physical existence, you are lost. The key is to stay in control of yourself and your destiny. Don't allow others to distract you from your path to greatness with their words or their actions.

I have been a Personal and Organizational Trainer for more than 25 years. I stumbled into this profession. My need for financial stability led me to an organization because I desired and needed more. I enrolled in school at Jackson State University, located in Jackson, Mississippi.

I was working on my Bachelor's degree full time and working a full-time job, as I mentioned earlier. As Les Brown says, I was hungry. Well, after about eight years of being a Manufacturing Supervisor, I decided to go back to school to work on a Master's degree in social work. I went into the office and turned in my two-week notice to my manager.

The plant manager called me into his office and stated that he needed me to help train the workforce of a new manufacturing facility they were starting up and would love to have my support to ensure they had a smooth startup. I agreed to stay on and train the workforce while working on my master's degree. One day, I ran into a former professor of mine from Jackson State University.

My former professor asked me what I had done since graduating. I explained to him that I was not working in the social work field, but I was a Manufacturing Supervisor. He said, "How are you doing at that?" I said, "I am doing well with it." He said, "Do you understand why?" I told him that I wasn't sure, but I felt that my social work education taught me how to connect with people and meet them where they are, to establish meaningful relationships.

He said, "You got it." He told me that a lot of supervisors and leaders fail because they do not understand this important piece. I walked away feeling better about my role. I had started feeling like I had wasted many years of my life attaining degrees that I was not using.

Now I could see that my degrees were much more beneficial in my role than I had realized. I graduated in 2000 with a Master of Social Work degree from Jackson State University. The company that I stayed on to support started up successfully.

I went from being a manufacturing technician to a manufacturing supervisor, to a quality assurance supervisor, which landed me the opportunity to become an area manager at another manufacturing facility.

I have been a manufacturing production trainer for over 25 years now. I am also a Certified Transformational Life Coach, a Manufacturing Global Training Expert, a motivational speaker, an entrepreneur, and now an author. I have taken my knowledge and training and put it into this book, to help people find their true purpose in life and learn to unlock their potential to achieve their dreams and live an abundant life.

People seek help for many reasons, such as recovery from a break-up or depression, or to break bad habits, just to name a few. Some of them seek counseling and others try to find ways of coping on their own. I believe taking the time to learn about ourselves and incorporating various coping strategies will lead to living better lives.

Social work involves a holistic model of analysis that considers the social, mental, and personally experienced problems of people through the lens of the person in the environment. It could be the work environment, the home environment, school environment, the neighborhood environment, etc.

Systems theories help us focus our thoughts on the interactions between people and their social and physical environments, and they help us to understand how change can occur using ecosystem interventions.

I touch on social work here because it helps us to explain the human experience and how people and their environments change.

Systems theory has continued to be important to social work thinking and practice as it provides a foundation for much of social work's understanding of human adaptation and coping in the face of adversity.

You see, our thoughts are very powerful, and learning how to change those thoughts can change our destiny.

As I was sitting and writing this book, a song came on that inspired my thoughts so much that I had to pause for a moment to reflect on all the good old days that helped shape me into the person I am today.

That artist is Gladys Knight and the song that stopped me in my tracks, mellowed the moment and brought a sensuous smile to my face, heart, mind, and soul is entitled *Memories*.

What music makes you pause for a moment and think about your actions and makes you want to do better and go after a change for the better?

Remember that our environment shapes our behavior but we must stay in control of our behavior within the environment.

I did not understand the power I had to change my paradigm, my way of life, by simply changing my way of thinking.

I became fascinated as I began seeing people change their lives and move past their current circumstances by simply reprogramming their minds and changing the way they looked at their lives and the things around them and taking action to move confidently in the direction of their dreams.

The true beauty is that the subconscious mind is adaptable and willing to change.

Imagine for a moment what you would do if you went over to a friend's house and they asked you to pass them a drink from the refrigerator. You would walk over to the refrigerator and pull the handle without thinking about your actions. You just know to pull the handle each time to open it, however, you probably cannot remember when you learned this, however each time you pull the handle, it opens.

This is because the information is stored in your subconscious mind.

So, if our subconscious mind has been operating on poor experiences and poor decision-making, it will provide you with continued poor decisions and unwise behaviors, which may lead you to additional undesirable behaviors and unfulfilled goals.

Sigmund Freud's psychoanalytic theory of personality argues that human behavior is the result of unconscious psychological conflicts shaping behavior and personality.

This is known as Freud's structural theory of personality, which emphasizes three parts of the mind: the id, ego, and superego.

By understanding how the subconscious mind works, you can learn how dreams become reality. The subconscious mind is a photographic mechanism in the brain. While the conscious mind sees an event, takes a picture of it, and remembers it, the subconscious works backward, seeing something before it happens. Understanding this means we can control the thoughts and images we feed it.

Trying hard, which may work for a task given to the conscious mind, is a cause of failure with the subconscious. The ease with which the subconscious accomplishes things increases with emotion. When a thought becomes a feeling and imagination desires, it will deliver what you want. English philosopher James Allen wrote, "As a man thinks, so he is, as he continues to think, so he remains."

Ralph Waldo Emerson wrote: "A man is what he thinks about all day long."

When we are unhappy, we try to remedy it by focusing on external factors we believe we need to change in order to create better circumstances; but this does not address the true root cause. Your thinking is often the driver behind why you feel the way you do.

Keep in mind that whatever you give your subconscious, it will register as fact. Believing it to be so can make a huge difference in how we live our lives.

By becoming aware and being in harmony with your subconscious mind, you can begin to take back control of your life. This is because when your subconscious and conscious mind work together to achieve a common goal, it's easy to believe that what you want will happen.

The id, superego, and ego are believed to be in constant conflict and adult personality and behavior are rooted in the results of these internal struggles throughout childhood.

Freud believed that a person who has a strong ego has a healthy personality and that imbalances in this system can lead to anxiety, depression, and unhealthy behaviors.

Alfred Adler was an Austrian medical doctor, psychotherapist, and founder of the school of individual psychology. He was the first to explore and develop a comprehensive social theory of the psychodynamic person and coined the idea of the "inferiority complex". The encyclopedia Britannica defines inferiority complex as, "a psychological sense of inferiority that is wholly or partly subconscious." Inferiority complex is also referred to as chronic low self-esteem. You call yourself names, focus on your shortcomings, and believe that your criticism of self is reasonable. Your self-esteem is very fragile and you constantly attack it. This cycle of belief consistently holds you back personally and professionally. We have to break this cycle of belief.

Let's consider your memory. To duplicate even in a minor way its storage capacity, I am reminded of how I heard someone explain that it would take several Congressional libraries, floor after floor of filing cabinets, and hundreds of trained librarians just to gather, separate, to fix, and classify the millions of images, incidents, impressions, experiences, and flashes of identification that you have collected through the years and which you can recall at will in fractions of a second.

This is only one of the God-given highly complicated systems, which is yours to use and to benefit from, at a moment's notice. It is a phenomenon of complicated ingenuity, and yet you take it as a matter of course and give it a second thought only when something happens to interfere with its perfection.

As you evaluate yourself, it might interest you to know that there is no one like you in the whole world. As a human being, you have your own unique physical and organic characteristics.

However, when we begin to compare, consider and evaluate personality, sensitivity, receptivity, mentality, adaptability, intelligence quotients, and potentialities, marked differences appear not only among people within the same general group or classification or among members of one family but even between identical twins.

This is where you become a distinct individual. As a matter of record, and phylogeny, as well as psychology, it has been substantiated that no two individuals are exactly alike in every respect.

In all the millions who lived before you, who are alive today and will be born in the future, there never has been and never will be anyone exactly like you. Nature and God have given you special talents, abilities, and aptitudes, which only you can use and develop.

You have never fully utilized those talents, those unique gifts of yours, for various reasons. You may have been too busy growing up, learning a trade, following a profession, raising a family, paying for a home, or meeting your obligations, and therefore never gave all your potentialities much of a chance. But what about now? Can you give attention to those hidden urges and let them find expression now? It is time for you to take courage and follow through on the desires of your heart. Your unique gifts and talents were never meant to be stifled, ignored, or forgotten. If you have the urge to sing, write, paint, travel, make things or learn something entirely new to you, go ahead and do it, do not hesitate, do it now. Your first attempts may be poor and discouraging but do not let it frighten you. Keep trying again and again for that in itself is an accomplishment. Find confidence in knowing that you are nature's greatest achievement, the most amazing and most complex form of life on earth. You are man created in the image of God and you can reach heights that you thought were unimaginable. So, I say to you, raise your head high and strive to do better every day as you climb onward and upward to your success where you are meant to find happiness and abundance.

The mind is the core of all human activity, the control center for all thought, feeling, emotion and reaction. Your mind is what you make of it.

Except for basic functional deficiencies or physical impairments, your brain can be trained and developed in numerous ways. It can grow, expand, project, deduce, combine, learn and remember. It can be directed into specialized channels and be conditioned to respond to strange stimuli. The creative "you" is that inner urge to find expression, recognition, and self-fulfillment. Behind it, lying asleep, are urges and potentialities within you that need only be tapped to open a new, glorious world of joy and satisfaction.

The imaginative "you" is the amazing ability of your mind to project itself into the unknown, the unexplored, and the unexpected.

It is in your capacity to dream; to envision new, entirely different, and seemingly impossible ways to do things, live, and make life more enjoyable. The conscious "you" is the reasoning, analytical "you" which enables you to compare, contrast, deduce, evaluate and come to certain decisions. That, however, is controlled by your emotions, which are the motivating power behind your behavior, your actions, and your reactions. They, in turn, are controlled by habit and it is within your power to change your habits to suit your desires.

The subconscious "you" is that vast, hidden, powerful force within you, as propounded originally by the father of psychiatry, Dr. Sigmund Freud.

He envisioned the unconscious as the repository of all dissatisfied urges and impulses, as the storehouse of all resentments, inhibitions, grievances, and frustrations. He saw the primacy of sex as the motivating force in the unconscious, as the representative of repressed and ungratified amoral desires. He maintained that the unconscious never forgot and never forgave for those repressions and claimed that unless it was diverted, through sublimation or transference, into constructive channels, it always exacted a toll on mental derangements. According to Freud, if left unchecked can lead to neurosis.

The important part to remember is that a physical illness or breakdown affects everything else about you. Your thoughts, your feelings, emotions, and even your outlook on life are influenced and colored by your physical condition.

A person who does not feel well, who is beset by pain or incapacitated by sickness, cannot be calm, composed and normal in his actions and reactions. He cannot be sociable, amiable, or considerate as usual. He cannot weigh facts properly or evaluate anything in his customary manner. If there is too much pain or discomfort, he cannot see or think straight. This affects his general behavior and his relationships with others.

Guard your health and it will help you obtain and retain a more sane, healthier outlook on life. It will also help you to be your natural, normal self. Too many of us like to appear important. We feel neglected when we are not the center of interest and at times will do almost anything to draw the desired attention to ourselves.

How about you? How often do you brag and boast about the importance of your job, your influential friends, your past, your activities in various groups, or other things? How often do you assume supercilious airs, convey the impression that you know all the answers, pretend you are too big to be bothered with petty things, or make-believe that money, as such, means nothing to you? How often do you seek recognition and would compromise yourself a dozen times, confidentially of course, to get a little publicity?

Have you ever stopped to ask yourself why you are so anxious to impress people? Psychologists say it is a form of anxiety and the basic reason for it lies in a feeling of inferiority. You want people to think that you are an important person. And so, you build the illusion that you have power, friends, and influence. Yet, at the same time, anxiety stays with you. You are constantly afraid that someone might look behind your false front and see you for what you are. So, you begin to brag and boast a little bit more. Titles, honors, badges of office, deference and prepaid servitudes have little meaning to the truly "big" man. He is above simple pretensions and petty subterfuges. He does not have to play a part or make-believe, and in most instances, he is a simple man. As for the little fellow, he thrives on those things. Many of us play a part, some of the time. We act one way at work and another at play. We may be kind and sweet at home but harsh and unyielding to those under us at work; we may be the life of the party at a social gathering and a surly, grumpy person at home; an overgenerous host when strangers are around but a penny-pincher in the bosom of our immediate family. Of course, a certain amount of play-acting is often required; call it polish, propriety, or company manners. We would like to tell the truth, to reveal our true feelings but we cannot do it for the moment and must be polite, friendly and solicitous. The danger lies in carrying pretense too far, in wearing the false front too long, in making believe too often. Then it becomes a form of escape and leads to trouble.

Dramatizing yourself too much, exaggerating every trivial incident, ascribing undue importance to petty things, and overacting on the slightest provocation are nerve-wracking. Pretending that you are somebody else and making a poor job of it is to undermine self-confidence, lose your own identity, and become a "nobody".

Pretense and dramatics may gain you temporary sympathy or attention but they seldom last and usually leave a bad taste in all concerned.

Guard your health and be your natural self. Capitalize upon what you have and what you are. Be simple, friendly, and pleasant. All of this will lighten your load, brighten your day and add to the joys, beauty, and richness of your life. In a sense, you are the product of your background, your experiences, and your environment. Some of it has been forced upon you and the rest is of your own making. This influence began in your infancy and has been at work ever since. It formed your likes and dislikes, molded your thoughts, engendered your beliefs, fostered your conclusions, and affected your actions and conditioned your responses.

It began with your parents and the members of your family, with your father's occupation and his love or hatred for it, with his contacts and affiliations at work and elsewhere, with his character and educational background, with your home surroundings and your mother's homemaking, with your family's status in the neighborhood and the community, with your parents' social and religious contacts, with what was said or discussed in your presence and with what you were encouraged to do or not to do. All of these had a tremendous influence on shaping your character, forming your concepts, and establishing your model of general behavior.

Later came your school years, your teachers and classmates, the friends you made, the work or profession you chose, the interests you developed, the mate you selected, the family you raised, and the standing you maintained. You were affected by the successes and failures you had, the disappointments you met, the grievances you nurtured, the social contacts you cultivated, and the leisure time activities you followed. These became the background and the pattern for your habitual reactions and in turn conditioned your beliefs and convictions.

This is true of you and all of us. As a result of such beliefs, feelings, and convictions, many of us are opinionated and prejudge others. Our minds are closed to changes or the slightest deviations from what we believe in and from what we approve of.

On the other hand, there are those among us who remain tolerant and open-minded; who leave room for a divergence in belief and opinion, and who make allowances for and accept differences in views, concepts, behavior, and conclusions.

So, how do we change our habits? When a given action is repeated so many times that it turns into a fixed tendency or an inclination and becomes almost automatic in its repetitive response it is called a habit.

"You can make your dreams come true. Just decide, then trust your subconscious mind to guide you there."
— **Anonymous Author.**

CHAPTER THIRTEEN

## Becoming Resilient and Driven
## (Staying focused on your true purpose)

*"Do not judge me by my success, judge me by how many times I fell down and got back up again."* —**Nelson Mandela**

**Stay focused on your true purpose.** Imagine you are at the end of your life and reflecting on all the places you traveled, all the people you met who brought you joy, all the things you accomplished, and then you realize that you forgot to do something. And now, you feel like you are not able to do it whether financially or health-wise. You begin to feel regret and your mind becomes consumed with how much you hate that you didn't get to experience it. Can you imagine how you would feel?

This is why it is important to write down what it is in this life that you want to do, want to accomplish, and mark it off as you do it or accomplish it. You have to strive for greatness and completeness. This is where my mindset is. Where is your mindset?

I choose to have no regrets when I get to the end of my life and sit outside rocking in a chair and waving at the people in their cars as they pass by. I want to reflect on my life, smile, and say, "Wow! I did everything on my list, what else can I add as a bonus?" Can you imagine the joy and level of personal fulfillment and accomplishment you would feel? The *Everyday Health* newsletter describes resilience as the ability to withstand adversity and bounce back from difficult life events. This does not mean that we don't experience stress, suffering, or emotional challenges but we have learned how to work through the emotional pain and suffering and find the mental capacity to bounce back.

So, no matter the challenges or adversity, find the courage to bounce back, review your list, take things off your list and keep smiling and keep moving toward your dream. I am reminded of Maya Angelou when she said, "I can be changed by what happens to me. But I refuse to be reduced by it."

And, I am reminded of Michelle Obama when she said, "Failure is an important part of your growth and developing resilience."

To be successful, you must want success earnestly, for it must be earned through tough self-discipline, continuous self-development, endless hard work, courageous perseverance, and complete dedication. Many fail to achieve because their hidden talents are never brought to light, developed and utilized. To get out the greatest that is in you, to succeed according to your God-given talents — that is life's greatest challenge, life's highest attainment, and life's most satisfying reward!

To help you find and uncover, strengthen and develop, gather and use the talents and powers dormant within you; to help you give your life direction and inspiring purpose — that is the committed purpose of this book. Know that you were born with your purpose; you simply have to find out what it is.

Success in life is a result of the decisions we make. You decide how much of yourself you want to unlock.

No matter what your age, man or woman, you can achieve greater success and happiness — a life truly worthwhile — if you will let this book be your guide.

We all go through challenges. What have you written on your list? What have you marked off on your list as accomplished or complete?

CHAPTER FOURTEENTH

# Celebrating You

*"When I stand before God at the end of my life, I would hope that I would not have a single bit of talent left, and could say, 'I used everything you gave me'"* —**Erma Bombeck**

I reached out to check on a friend that I had not communicated with for quite some time. I texted, "Hello, just texting to see how you are doing, you were on my mind." My friend texted back and said, "I guess I am okay, just taking one day at a time." Then she texts, "How are you?" I replied, "I am doing well and feeling blessed. I have learned to appreciate the days when I have calmness of mind." She texted back and said, "Thanks, you are so right, believe me, I have seen times that I had so much on my mind that I could not even sleep for the thoughts." She said, "How quickly we forget or look over our blessings." She sent a smile emoji, one of a heart and another text that read, "Thanks for reminding me." We both were inspired by our communication.

There is so much more we can have in life, but we settle for some reason. We get so caught up in thinking about the bad things that we overlook all the good we have experienced. We forget how resilient we have become because of the challenges we have faced. We forget to take the time to celebrate and appreciate how strong and wise we are after coming out of the storms of life.

Here, the fae that brings fear is clearer than the goal. It is unimportant, subordination, and low status without freedom. It is being, to one's knowledge, a no-account person, having to lead a confined life in inferior circumstances, a weak, anxious, boring life, doing unimportant and dull things, and passing out of this world as if one may very well have never come into it.

I hope you have decided not to settle anymore and aspire to seek understanding on how important it is to continue pushing past your fears and celebrate yourself. Pat yourself on the back!

Make a commitment to begin each day with prayer and meditation. Through prayer we seek our higher power's blessings, pay our gratitude and ask for patience and strength to bear the trials of life. Through meditation, we can begin to take charge of our minds.

Meditation is a spiritual activity in which a person uses techniques to train their attention and obtain increased awareness of themselves and their surroundings.

Write your vision down.

Your vision defines "your" what to do. It gives you a clear idea of where you are going. It should be your source of motivation.

Begin surrounding yourself with positive, like-minded people and finding the motivation to continue moving toward your destiny.

You will begin to see yourself attaining what you rightfully deserve for yourself and your family.

Take control of your thoughts and feelings. You have this ability. Practice self-love. We all want to know the steps to take to get where we want to be in life. But many just don't know how to shift their mindset to create the change they desire.

You have the power and ability to change your thoughts and beliefs. Remember, it is our thoughts and feelings that create the actions, and it is through our actions we achieve the results that we seek.

I take great joy in seeing others live the life they have dreamed about. I teach others how to unlock their lives by learning how to control their thoughts and behavior. It is through strategic steps and analysis that we help others achieve outcomes they value.

Read and reread each paragraph in this book and give yourself time to digest and absorb its contents, and if some particular passage strikes you or applies specifically to your needs, underline it.

Then, and only then, will you begin to look inward, evaluate your direction, explore and examine your problems, understand the reasons for your disturbances and begin to learn how to gradually eliminate many of your fears, anxieties, worries, and frustrations. This will give you the courage and understanding to push past them in pursuit of your unique greatness.

Recognize that this is the beginning of a whole new life for you and you have already taken the first step forward and upward at this very moment.

Your new life is in your awareness that there are disturbing factors in your present emotional make-up. It is in your desire to look for the contributory causes and begin to eliminate them. It is in your reading and understanding of the content and in your willingness to follow through with your plan for success in the days to come.

It is in your readiness to study, learn, and use ideas suggested to the best of your ability. Begin by evaluating yourself and realizing that you are something unique in this world of ours.

Here, in a nutshell, are the ingredients of a practical and attainable system for success and happiness — the fullest possible growth and utilization of your physical, mental, and spiritual resources; an inspiring purpose worthy of your talents; a blue-print for intelligent action; a deep and burning desire to achieve your objective; and an unshakable will to never give up.

Agree to receive it undeniably with all your enthusiasm — "Nothing great," said Emerson, "was ever achieved without enthusiasm." Talk it up to yourself.

Thomas J. Watson, Sr. reminds us that: "The great accomplishments of man have resulted from the transmission of ideas and enthusiasm."

Winston Churchill reminds us that: "Success consists of going from failure to failure without loss of enthusiasm."

Nelson Mandela reminds us that: "There is no passion to be found playing small- In settling for a life that is less than the one you are capable of living."

Remind yourself, over and over again, of your imagination, inner passion, desires, strengths and visions. Keep moving in that direction in spite of challenges and setbacks. Become unstoppable!

And, day after day take actions to elevate your life with the success and happiness you so solemnly desire. Amplify and maximize your potential by using your power to succeed. You have all you need, it has already been given to you by the Almighty.

You have the potential to do even more than you imagined. Trust and believe that you can. Commit yourself to begin living the life you were meant to live. Avail yourself of your power to unlock your life and unlock your dreams.

**"Don't Count the Days; Make the Days Count."** Muhammad Ali

# About the Author

**Shirley Brown Danzy**
*Motivational speaker, author, and mindset coach*

Shirley Brown Danzy is an author, motivational speaker, and mindset coach based in the state of Mississippi. She has a passion for helping people unlock the full potential of their lives for a broader tomorrow. In addition to that, Shirley is also a motivational speaker and Mindset Coach who operates with the aim of motivating people to find their inner strength and the right self-confidence to overcome challenges and struggles through life. With a diverse career spanning over two decades in management, leadership, and social work, Shirley has embraced her purpose as someone who was put on this Earth to help others become true achievers and unlock the full potential of their dreams. She strongly believes that anybody has the power within, and it is really all about harnessing such power and using it to channel positivity and growth in their lives.

Find out more about Shirley Brown Danzy:
https://www.linkedin.com/in/shirley-brown-danzy-99b12b10a

**Shirley Brown Danzy**

# More About the Author

Shirley Brown Danzy was born in the small town of Crystal Springs, Mississippi and spent most of her formative years there. She spent the remainder of her early years in Subdivision Number 2, a Westside community in Hinds County. She attended Jackson State University, where she attained bachelor's and master's degrees in Social Work, and she is presently pursuing a PhD in Social Work from the same university.

Shirley is currently a Global Trainer for a Major Corporation and has previously worked with vulnerable children and adults who have suffered from abuse and neglect. Her enduring aim is to succeed and it was this drive that made her think about how she could help others to do the same.

The answer was to begin by writing her first book, **The Power to Succeed**, in which she provides readers with the tools they will need to achieve whatever level of success they are aiming for through a combination of self-belief, developing the right mindset and building resilience, among other positive traits.

In her free time, Shirley loves traveling, spending time with her family, relaxing on her back porch and enjoying the great outdoors. Above all else, Shirley enjoys helping other people to reach for their personal and professional goals and showing them the ways to achieve them, no matter how big or small they may be.

Shirley is a member of the National Association of Social Workers (NASW), which offers an array of programs and opportunities that enhance the well-being of individuals, families, and communities through the advancement of social work policy and practice.

She is also a member of The Mary S. Nelums Foundation, which awards scholarships to deserving social work students who display a strong commitment and dedication to excellence in social work practice.

"Every day is a chance to begin again. Don't focus on the failures of yesterday, start today with the positive thoughts and expectation."
**—Catherine Pulsifer**

In Loving Memory of my Dad
**John D Brown**

Please join my online community by visiting www.shirleybrowndanzy.com, you will have access to self-development exercises, exclusive file downloads, first opportunity to purchase new products and register for upcoming speaking engagements, as well as many other amazing benefits and opportunities.

**And, because you have purchased this book, access to one free e-book is being offered for a limited time after the launch of this book.** To take advantage of this life-changing opportunity, please go to my website, click on the free e-book Icon and get started on unlocking your full potential. The e-book has been designed to be used in conjunction with this book, "The Power to Succeed: Unlock Your Life, Unlock Your Dreams."

Hope to see you there!

For more information and more resources you can connect with me further at the following locations:

Facebook: https://m.facebook.com/?_rdr

Instagram: https://www.instagram.com/authorshirleybrowndanzy

Email: Shirley@shirleybrowndanzy.com

Website: https://www.shirleybrowndanzy.com

# Note Pages–My Plan for Success

www.ingramcontent.com/pod-product-compliance
Lightning Source LLC
Chambersburg PA
CBHW050254120526
44590CB00016B/2344